# Holding on to Hope

By Muneer Tawam

Illustrated by Cafeconlecheart

My name is Amal and I'm only eight.
I was born in Gaza
under an apartheid state.

I'm surrounded by walls
and wired gates.

They call it an open air prison
but I'm innocent I swear.

I just want to draw
and braid my doll's hair.

I just want to sleep
without any nightmares
but that's just a dream
because life isn't fair.

I wake up to the sound of bombs
and voices in despair.

I want to help so bad
but what can I do?

I'm just a little kid
with a brother who is only two.

His name is Ahmad and he doesn't
have a clue why we don't have food,
water, electricity or a home to go
back to.

It wasn't always this way.
We had a house of our own, a place
where we could stay.

We had family gatherings
where we would laugh and play.

My dad was a fisherman
he would take me out to sea.

As the sun was glistening over my
father and me, I would stare into
the distance imagining what the
future will be.

I miss harvesting olives with my beautiful mother. She was the rock of our family, kept us grounded like no other.

My neighbors are monsters
they are unjust.

They bombed every institution
turning it to dust.

What's the solution
for someone like me?

I'm not asking for much
just a place to be free.

I want a room of my own
a yard with a tree.

But who am I kidding?
I'm just a refugee.

The world has turned it's back
and that's clear as can be.

My people are on track
of the right side of history.

I'm holding on to hope
even though it's very slippery.

One day I will cope
with all of this misery.

Until that day comes
I am still here.

I have to stay strong
and hold back my tears.

I am physically in danger
every single year
but my soul is liberated
I have no fear.

Once we are free
from the river to the sea
we can all go home and
turn our rightful key.

This book is dedicated to the children of Gaza. We will never turn our back on you. We hear you loud and clear, and we will continue to echo your voices. Your bravery and resilience is an inspiration to anyone who has a heart. Please hold onto hope, as the future will bring a brighter day for you and your children one day.

A special thank you to my good friend and dear brother, Ramsey Abdallah, for inspiring the idea for this book. Without you reaching out to me this book would not come into fruition.

All the love,
Muneer Tawam

Muneer understands the plight of the Palestinian people, as he is the child of Palestinian immigrants who moved to the United States to escape life under occupation. The subject of this book really hits home for him, as he still has family in Palestine and is frequently concerned for their safety. He is also the author of Generation Tech and the Four Seasons, which was written as a memento to his four boys.

# Glossary

## A

**Amal:** name of Arabic origin which means "hope".
**Apartheid:** a policy of keeping people of different races separate and unequal in a society.

## C

**Cope:** to handle or deal with in a successful way.

## D

**Despair:** the complete lack of hope.
**Distance:** the measure of space between things, places, or points in time.

## G

**Glistening:** to shine or sparkle with reflected light.

## H

**Harvesting:** the gathering of ripe crops, the crops or the amount of crops gathered, or the season in which they are gathered.

# I

**Innocent:** free from evil or knowledge of evil.

**Institution:** an organization set up for a specific purpose, usually serving the public. Hospitals, churches, prisons, and schools can be institutions.

# L

**Liberated:** to free or let out.

# M

**Misery:** a condition in which one is very unhappy, in need, or suffers very much.

# P - R

**Physically:** in, with, or by means of the body.

**Refugee:** a person forced to leave his or her home or country to seek safety or protection.

**Rightful:** having a legal or legitimate claim.

# S - U

**Solution:** an answer to or explanation of a problem.

**Unjust:** contrary to the principles of fairness or justice.

# Palestine

Gaza

Four Sons Publishing
www.foursonspublishing.com
Copyright© 2024 by Muneer Tawam
All rights reserved.

www.ingramcontent.com/pod-product-compliance
Lightning Source LLC
Chambersburg PA
CBHW060835270326
41933CB00002B/92